Anne Frank

Vanora Leigh

Illustrations by Richard Hook

Wayland

Great Lives

William Shakespeare
Queen Elizabeth II
Anne Frank
Martin Luther King
Helen Keller
Ferdinand Magellan
Mother Teresa
Louis Braille
John Lennon
John F. Kennedy

First published in 1985 by
Wayland (Publishers) Limited
49 Lansdowne Place, Hove
East Sussex BN3 1HF, England

ISBN 0 85078 564 2

Phototypeset by Kalligraphics Ltd, Redhill, Surrey
Printed in Italy by G. Canale & C.S.p.A., Turin
Bound in the U.K. by The Pitman Press, Bath

Contents

A special diary

In the summer of 1942, a young Jewish schoolgirl, living in Amsterdam, received a very special thirteenth birthday present – a diary. It was special for her because it became a close friend, in whom she could confide.

For the rest of the world, too, this diary became very special, when it was published five years later. It made that schoolgirl's name – Anne Frank – famous throughout the world.

Anne's account of how she, her family and four friends hid from the Nazis for two years, became a bestseller. More, it came to represent the suffering and persecution of all Jewish people during the Second World War.

Sadly, this talented young girl, who would surely have become a great writer, died in a concentration camp when she was fifteen. Perhaps the most famous words in her diary were: 'I want to go on living after my death. And therefore I am grateful to God for giving me this gift . . . of expressing all that is in me.' Today, through her diary, Anne does live on – in people's hearts and minds.

Early childhood

Anne Frank was born on 12th June 1929, in Frankfurt-on-Main in Germany. Her parents both came from wealthy Jewish families who had lost their money during the First World War. The Franks had one other daughter, Margot, who was three years older than Anne.

In 1933, Adolf Hitler became Chancellor of Germany. He believed that the German people were Aryans and that the Aryan race was the strongest and best in the world. All other races, he thought, were inferior, especially the Jews.

Within a year of Hitler's coming to power, concentration camps were filling up, first with his political opponents, and later with everyone who disagreed with him or who were regarded as 'inferior', including gypsies and Jews.

The Frank family left Germany for the safety of Holland in 1933. They settled in Amsterdam, where Mr Frank established a wholesale business in herbs and spices. For a few years, the family lived in peace and comfort.

The Frank family moved from Germany to Holland to escape Nazi persecution, which included burning Jewish synagogues.

What life was like for the Jews

This Jewish family, living under the German occupation of Holland, have been turned out of their home.

Until May 1940, life in Holland for the country's estimated 14,000 Jews was free from official anti-semitism (persecution against Jews). But this soon changed after the Germans arrived.

With the German occupation of Holland, persecution of Jews became official policy. All Jews, even children, had to wear a yellow six-pointed star on their clothing, to distinguish them. They were not allowed to ride on trams, and had to hand in their bicycles.

Their social life was severely restricted. Visits to the theatre, cinema and all sports grounds, were forbidden. They had to do all their shopping at Jewish shops between the hours of 3.00 and 5.00 p.m. and their children had to attend Jewish schools. They could not visit their Christian friends, and they had to be indoors by 8.00 p.m. every evening – even sitting in their gardens after that time was forbidden. But life, somehow, did go on. 'Our freedom was strictly limited. Yet things were still bearable,' wrote Anne, in her diary.

Anne at school

Anne seemed to be a happy, friendly girl who enjoyed playing ping pong and eating ice cream, and who boasted that she had 'strings of boyfriends'. Yet underneath, as she admitted to her beloved diary, she was very lonely and longed to find a 'real' friend. In fact her diary, which she always called Kitty, became her closest friend.

At school, Anne was an intelligent pupil. Unfortunately, her great weakness was talking in class and several times, as a punishment, her teacher made her write essays with titles such as 'A Chatterbox' and 'Incurable Chatterbox'. Anne even nicknamed herself Miss Quack Quack! But, despite the chattering, Anne still managed to achieve excellent exam results at the Jewish Secondary School she attended.

Outside school, thirteen-year-old Anne was beginning to show an interest in boys, who obviously found her an attractive and lively girl. Only a week before she and her family were forced into hiding, she invited a boy home to meet her parents and enjoy a tea of cream cakes.

Into hiding

What Jews feared most during the German occupation was to receive a call-up notice from the Gestapo. Officially, this meant that they had to register for work, but, as most Jews knew, it really meant that they were to be arrested and taken away to concentration camps.

At the beginning of July 1942, sixteen-year-old Margot Frank was sent a call-up notice. The thought of her sister being taken away terrified Anne. For the first time she heard her parents talk about going into hiding. 'Where would they go?' she wondered. 'When, and how?'

Soon the girls were told to pack their most vital belongings into a satchel. Anne chose her hair curlers, handkerchiefs, school books, a comb, old letters – and her diary. She admitted they were the craziest things: 'But I'm not sorry, memories mean more to me than dresses.'

Dutch friends came to take away spare clothes and then Anne had to say goodbye to her little cat, who was given to some kind neighbours.

Jewish victims of Nazi persecution being transported to a concentration camp.

They left the house in an untidy state – breakfast things on the table, unmade beds, meat left out for the cat – so that people would believe they had left in a desperate hurry and had, perhaps, fled the country.

It was raining as the family made their way through the Amsterdam streets and they were glad it was a cool day. They were all wearing as much clothing as possible because it would have looked suspicious to carry suitcases. Anne wore two vests, three pairs of knickers, a dress, skirt, jacket, summer coat, two pairs of stockings, lace-up shoes and a woolly cap and scarf. People looked at them sympathetically, but because they were wearing the yellow stars that proclaimed them Jews, no-one dared to offer them a lift.

At last, Anne was told where they were going. They were heading for a secret hideaway to which her father had been sending provisions. They were going to disappear inside the building where Mr Frank had his office. Here, they hoped, no German would ever think of searching for them.

9

The hiding place

The building where Otto Frank worked was an ancient, narrow house, overlooking the Prinsengracht (Princes' Canal).

On the ground floor of the old house was a warehouse, used as a store. The front door to the house was next to the store and inside was an inner door leading to a staircase. At the top of the stairs, the main office and a smaller room, containing a safe, led to a second office. From there, a long passage led past the coal store into a private office with a lavatory and kitchen. Wooden stairs led from the downstairs passage to the next floor. At the top was a small landing with a door at each end, one leading to attics at the front of the house, and the other door, to the hideaway or, as Anne called it, 'our secret annexe'. A few days after the Frank family arrived, a moveable bookcase was placed in front of the door to conceal it.

The house on Prinsengracht today. The 'secret annexe' was upstairs, at the back of the house.

Making a 'home'

Much preparation had gone into planning the secret annexe. The Frank family had a bedsitting room with a small bedroom next door for the two girls. Next to this was a room with a washbasin and lavatory. Up a flight of stairs were a large room with a cooking stove and a tiny corridor room. These two rooms were for another Jewish family, the Van Daans. An attic, which was to become a very special place for Anne, completed the number of rooms.

During the first day, Anne and her father unpacked all the boxes of provisions which lay piled on the floor. Next day they scrubbed and cleaned the rooms. Anne tried to make the walls of her little room look less bare by pasting up pictures of film stars.

One of the first tasks was to sew loose strips of material into makeshift curtains. These were to make sure that no neighbours would see or hear them. The curtains were fixed into position with drawing pins, 'not to come down until we emerge from here', said Anne.

The other occupants

Soon after the Franks moved into the secret annexe, they were joined by Mr and Mrs Van Daan, fifteen-year-old Peter, and his cat Mouschi. Anne was not impressed with Peter and thought him 'a rather soft, shy gawky youth'. Her feelings about him were to change completely during the two years they shared their cramped accommodation, but not her opinion of his mother.

Mrs Van Daan thought Anne a spoilt chattering girl. For her part, Anne regarded Mrs Van Daan, or Madame as she sometimes referred to her, as pushy, selfish, cunning and discontented. Mrs Van Daan did most of the cooking in the annexe and, according to Anne, always made sure she had the choicest portions of food at mealtimes. Arguments were frequent in the Van Daan family, especially when Mrs Van Daan learnt she would have to sell her fur coat to raise money.

Anne's relationship with Mr Van Daan was little better. She thought him selfish and opinionated. Yet, although Anne relished the challenge of an argument with Mrs Van Daan, she thought it best not to answer back to Mr Van Daan. 'Oh, he can spit like a cat – I'd rather not argue . . .' she admitted.

In November 1942, the eighth member of the secret annexe 'family' moved in, a dentist called Albert Dussel. Anne's first thoughts were that he was a nice man – this was fortunate as he was to share her room in Margot's place (Margot moved in with her parents). Soon, however, Anne discovered that Mr Dussel was every bit as selfish and argumentative as Mr and Mrs Van Daan. When he was not eating, he was either dozing or working at the shared table in their shared room. One of Anne's greatest domestic battles – and, with her father's aid, greatest victories – was to persuade Dussel, or 'His Lordship', as she called him, to let her use the table to study on for a few extra hours a week.

Anne and Mr Dussel argue over who should have the use of the table for studying.

The lifeline

The families living in hiding in the annexe would have had little chance of survival without outside help. Even though they knew they would be severely punished by the Germans if they were caught, a small group of courageous Dutch people provided a necessary lifeline for Anne and the other hideaways.

These brave people included former employees of Mr Frank; Mr Koophuis and Mr Kraler, Miep Van Senten, Elli Vossen, and Miep's husband Henk. Elli's father worked in the warehouse below the annexe. When he was told about the hiding place, he offered to help and actually made the moveable bookcase which so

successfully concealed the door leading into the annexe.

Working as a team, the Dutch group provided the hideaways with fresh food. This was bought either on the black market or with food stamps obtained through the underground network of Dutch people pledged to help those, like the Franks, to hide from the Germans. The hideaways suffered at mealtimes if Miep or Elli were unable to shop for them: once they were reduced to eating a horrible-tasting vegetable stew because their helpers were unable to bring them fresh food.

The Dutch helpers also provided the hideaways with clothes, books, magazines – and brought gossip and news about the world outside the annexe. And all the time they risked their own lives by doing so. On one occasion a Gestapo car accidentally ran into Miep as she was carrying forbidden books for Mr Dussel. Yet, as Anne noted in her diary, they never complained or showed fear. '. . . although others may show heroism in the war or against the Germans, our helpers display heroism in their cheerfulness and affection.'

Life in the Annexe

For two years, the occupants of the annexe lived their lives within five small rooms. They never left these rooms, except to visit other parts of the building when the offices below were empty. No wonder they often argued and even Anne admitted she sometimes felt tearful and depressed. During weekdays, when the building was occupied, they had to be completely silent, and spent much of the time creeping around, not daring to cough, laugh or use the lavatory.

Anne described in her diary a typical day in the life of the annexe and the strict routine the hideaways had developed to keep their hiding-place secret. The day started at 6.45 a.m., when Mr Van Daan was first up and into the bathroom. People began arriving for work at the warehouse at 8.30 a.m. and after that there had to be complete silence in the annexe. While Anne ate her breakfast of

The hideaways were always interested to hear news from outside.

porridge, her father was last in line for the bathroom. After the workers arrived there could be no water run or any moving about. The hideaways then read, sewed or talked quietly.

The sound of Mrs Van Daan's vacuum cleaner on her one precious carpet signalled that it was 12.30 p.m., when the warehouse workers went home. While Mrs Van Daan and Mrs Frank prepared lunch, the rooms would often fill with welcome visitors – Miep and her husband Henk, Elli, Mr Kraler or Mr Koophuis. At 1.00 p.m. everyone was silent again, to listen to the BBC on their secret radio.

During lunch, of soup and pudding, the outside helpers would relate the up-to-date news from outside. Silence reigned again in the afternoon, when Anne would study shorthand or read stories of Greek and Roman mythology. She had to compete for a share of the table in her room with Mr Dussel. At 5.30 p.m. the warehouse workers went home and there was freedom for the rest of the evening for the hideaways.

17

A time for relaxing

Now that it was evening, the outside helpers would arrive. Very often it would be Elli who came, and she would be given something to eat before receiving her shopping list. Mrs Van Daan frequently wanted various little items and, as she listed all the requests, Elli would wink at Anne.

After Elli left, Anne would often go down into the offices below to have a look around. The others would also go down there; Mr Van Daan would look through the day's post, Anne's father, whom she nicknamed Pim, would carry the typewriter upstairs to do some work, and Margot would find a quiet spot to study her

shorthand course. Dinner, prepared by Mrs Van Daan and Mrs Frank, would be served at some time during the evening, depending on when there was a news broadcast. At these times, all the inhabitants of the annexe would huddle around their secret radio, listening to news of what was going on in the outside world.

By 9.00 p.m. everyone was making preparations for bed. This was quite a complicated business.

'Nothing remains where it is during the day,' wrote Anne. Chairs were moved about, folding beds brought down from the walls, and blankets distributed.

The bathroom routine followed again and Anne would clean her teeth, manicure her nails and put her hair up in curlers. Very occasionally, she admitted in her diary, a flea would be found floating in the washing water.

Living with fear

The hideaways lived in constant fear of discovery by the Gestapo.

On several occasions the building was broken into by burglars. The families' greatest fear was that these burglars might discover their hiding place and tell the police. Then the Gestapo would come and they would all be captured and sent to concentration camps somewhere in Europe.

One frightening incident happened on the evening of Easter Sunday 1944, when the hideaways heard sounds of someone trying to break in. The men rushed downstairs; Mr Van Daan, forgetting the silence, shouted 'police'. Just when they thought the burglars had fled, a married couple passed the building and saw a hole in the front door made by the intruders. Believing that the couple would notify the police, the annexe families hid in the darkness of their rooms, hardly daring to breathe. They heard footsteps in the building and someone rattled the bookcase concealing the door to the annexe.

'During that night I really felt that I had to die,' Anne wrote. 'I waited for the police, I was prepared as the soldier is on the battlefield.'

Not all gloom

Although life in the annexe was often grim, there were celebrations when everyone tried to forget their circumstances and enjoy themselves. Birthdays, anniversaries and Jewish festivals were always celebrated. The outside helpers would try to bring little extras, such as flowers and sweets, for the hideaways to give as gifts.

Anne spent two birthdays in the annexe. On her fourteenth birthday she received sweets and a big book on her favourite subject, Greek and Roman mythology. The following birthday she was given lots of presents, including new underclothes, some jam, a ginger cake, two bottles of yoghurt and three slices of cream cheese.

Their day-to-day food was often poor and indigestible, so extra food was always a treat. During her last Christmas in the annexe, Anne made sweets for Miep and Elli, from sugar saved from her ration. Even sour Mr Dussel presented Mrs Van Daan and Mrs Frank with a special cake, baked by Miep.

How Anne spent her days

Although there were times when Anne felt unhappy and frustrated, she kept herself busy and filled her days with reading and writing. Besides keeping her diary, she also wrote short stories.

One of her favourite hobbies was compiling family trees, particularly those of the royal families of Europe.

She kept up with her school studies and especially enjoyed history, art and music, but had '. . . a great loathing for algebra, geometry and figures.' As well as learning French and reading books in English, she, together with Margot and Peter, also took a postal course in shorthand, which was ordered for them by Elli. Margot and Anne were given a lot of office work to do by Elli. '. . . it makes us both feel quite

important and is a great help to her,' Anne wrote.

Anne's great ambition was to be a writer or journalist and eventually to travel to cities such as Paris and London, to study the art and learn the languages. She never seemed to think that one day she and her family might be caught – her one worry was that when the war ended, she would be too far behind with her school work.

Like any other girl of her age, Anne loved experimenting with hairstyles, and she liked new clothes. Unfortunately these were in short supply. One day she decided to make herself a pretty dance frock from an old petticoat belonging to her mother. She went through a craze for dancing and ballet and practised her steps every evening, finding that this helped her stiff legs to become supple again.

Perhaps what Anne loved to do more than anything else was to go into the attic and watch the sky from the open window. 'As long as this exists and I may live to see it, this sunshine, the cloudless skies, while this lasts, I cannot be unhappy,' she told her diary.

Falling in love

During the first few months that Anne knew Peter Van Daan she complained that he was moody, lazy and worried too much about his health. She even nicknamed him, sarcastically, 'M'lord.' Yet Anne was also very lonely and needed a friend to whom she could confide. 'Somehow or other I took it into my head to choose Peter,' she wrote.

The families had been sharing the Annexe for eighteen months before the friendship between Anne and Peter became close.

Soon the two were spending a lot of time together. By now, Anne was more of a young woman than a girl and Peter, at seventeen, felt very protective towards her. Anne, for her part, felt that Peter ' . . . is a first rate chap, too, just like Daddy!'

The deepening friendship between Anne and Peter gave them both a taste of happiness in their upstairs prison. It was an important relationship in Anne's life – one that lasted for little more than six short months.

The world outside the annexe

Conditions were harsh for the Dutch people under the German occupation.

Although they were in hiding, the occupants of the annexe were always able to keep in touch with what was happening in the war-torn world outside.

News came to them from their helpers and through their radio. They learnt that their Jewish friends were being rounded up by the Gestapo and transported to concentration camps. And they heard that the furniture had been stripped from their homes, that burglaries were commonplace, that people had to queue for food, that the Dutch people were hungry and cold.

The radio informed them about the progress of the war. 'Hungary is occupied by German troops. There are still a million Jews there, so they too will have had it now . . .', Anne commented bleakly in her diary. But hearing the voice of the British Prime Minister, Winston Churchill, always cheered her up.

Living in the centre of Amsterdam, the hideaways also heard and saw allied bombers flying overhead and bombs being dropped on the city.

Last days

The hideaways followed the progress of the Allied landings in France on their radio.

Hopefulness brimmed over in the annexe during the spring of 1944. In everyone's mind was the belief that the allied forces would invade Europe any day. The thought of leaving the annexe caused Anne to think about the many months she had spent indoors, barely glimpsing the outside world through a window.

'. . . I regard our hiding as a dangerous adventure, romantic and interesting . . .' she wrote. And she thought about her future once she was free, of how she would lead a different and more exciting life than other girls. She felt at peace with everyone – including the Van Daans and Mr Dussel! '. . . how beautiful nature is, how good the people are about me, how interesting this adventure is! Why, then, should I be in despair?'

On 6th June, the occupants of the secret annexe heard the news they had been waiting for on their radio. 'This is D-day', came the

26

announcement. The invasion had begun. Anne followed its course closely. She thought the war would soon be over and longed to return to school again.

The others in the annexe also thought about what they would do once they were free. Margot and Mr Van Daan wanted a long, hot bath; Mrs Van Daan dreamed of cream cakes, while Peter said he would go straight to the cinema.

Mr Dussel hoped to see his wife again; Mr Frank wanted to visit business friends, and Mrs Frank longed for a cup of fresh coffee.

Although they had very little fresh food, towards the end of their time in the annexe, the hideaways were given twenty-four trays of fresh strawberries. They laughed and joked as they bottled the fruit and made strawberry jam. 'For two whole days, strawberries and nothing but strawberries,' Anne wrote.

No sooner were the strawberries finished than Anne was asked to help shell a supply of fresh peas, sent to them by a local greengrocer. Anne liked peas, '. . . but oh the work . . . uh!'

Discovery

On 1st August 1944, Anne wrote the last entry in her diary. Three days later, German Security Police, accompanied by Dutch Nazis, raided the main office and forced Mr Kraler to reveal the secret annexe. All the occupants were arrested and their valuables were seized. The contents of Mr Frank's attaché case, including Anne's notebooks, were scattered on the floor.

The prisoners were first sent to Westerbork, the main German

concentration camp in Holland. Later they were transferred in cattle trucks, eastward to Auschwitz, the terrible camp in German-occupied Poland. Here Mrs Frank died of starvation and Mr Van Daan was gassed. Mr Dussel died in another camp and Peter Van Daan was carried off with the Germans, when they were forced to evacuate Auschwitz as the Russian forces approached. He was never heard of again.

Anne, Margot and Mrs Van Daan were all sent from Auschwitz to another concentration camp, Belsen in Germany. Anne's qualities of courage and endurance never left her despite the cruelty and misery around her.

Mrs Van Daan was first to die in Belsen. In February 1945, both sisters caught typhus. One day, Margot, who was lying in the bunk above Anne, tried to get up, lost her grip and fell to the floor. She died from the shock of the fall. A few days later, in early March, Anne, too, died. It has been said that Margot's death did to Anne what all her previous sufferings had failed to do – it finally broke her spirit.

The only survivor from the eight in the annexe was Mr Frank, who was liberated from Auschwitz by Russian troops. He went back to Amsterdam where he met Miep and Elli again. They gave him Anne's precious notebooks – her diary – which had been handed to them by an office cleaner who found them shortly after the German raid on the annexe.

The forbidding gateway to one of the Nazis' infamous concentration camps. This picture was taken after the liberation by Allied forces.

Postscript

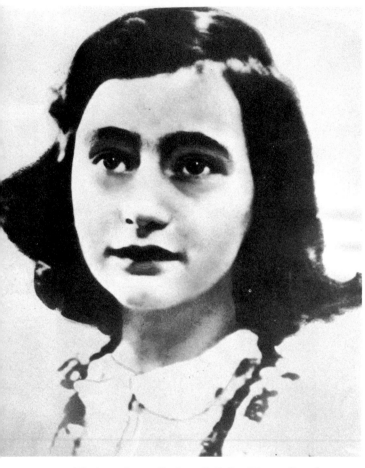

Friends advised Mr Frank that his daughter's diary should be published. It first appeared in 1947, under the title *The Annexe*, a name chosen by Anne herself. Since its first appearance, more than 13 million copies of *The Diary of Anne Frank*, in over fifty languages, have been printed. A stage play and a film have also been made of the book.

Today the house where Anne and the others lived is a museum run by the Anne Frank Foundation, which was set up in 1957. There you can see the little rooms in the annexe where eight people lived, laughed and argued for two years in hiding. The stove on which they cooked their food is still there and, most poignant of all, the photographs of film stars which Anne pasted on to the walls of her room to make it look brighter.

The main aim of the Anne Frank Foundation is to preserve the annexe, but it also works to continue Anne's struggle for a better world, where discrimination against people of a different culture or different skin colour, no longer exists.

Dates

1929 Anne's birth
1933 The family move to Amsterdam from Frankfurt
1939 Outbreak of the Second World War
1940 German invasion of Holland
1942 The family go into hiding
1944 Capture
1945 Anne's death

New words

Allied Forces The armed services of the forty-nine countries allied against Germany, Italy and Japan in the Second World War. The allies included Great Britain, the United States, Russia, the Commonwealth countries, France.

Anti-Semitism Discrimination and persecution of Jewish people.

Aryans A race of people believed by the Nazis to be the 'master race', with no mixture of Jewish blood. Also called Nordic race.

Black market The illegal buying and selling of goods in violation of official controls.

Concentration camps Guarded prison camps set up by the Nazis, to which people who disagreed with the regime were sent. In addition, it was official Nazi policy to eliminate all the Jewish people, by sending them to concentration camps where huge numbers were starved to death or killed by gas.

D-day The day selected for the Allied invasion of Europe – 6th June 1944.

Gestapo The secret state police of Nazi Germany.

Nazis Members of Adolf Hitler's National Socialist German Workers' Party.

Persecution Bullying and ill-treatment, especially because of race or religion.

Typhus A serious illness often brought on by bad diet and dirty living conditions.

Books to read

Anne Frank by Angela Bull (Hamish Hamilton, 1984)

The Age of Upheaval: The World since 1914 by J.M. Roberts (Penguin Books, 1981)

The Diary of Anne Frank (Pan Books, 49th printing 1982)

The Footsteps of Anne Frank by Ernst Schnabel (Pan Books, 1981)

Picture credits

BBC Hulton 25; Colorpix 10; Imperial War Museum/Wayland 26; Popperfoto 25; Wayland Picture Library 1, 6, 9, 29. Cover artwork by Richard Hook.

Index